47

WAYS TO LOSE YOUR MONEY DAY TRADING

COSTLY MISTAKES EVERY BEGINNER MAKES

"This book is based on my experience during my first year of trading.

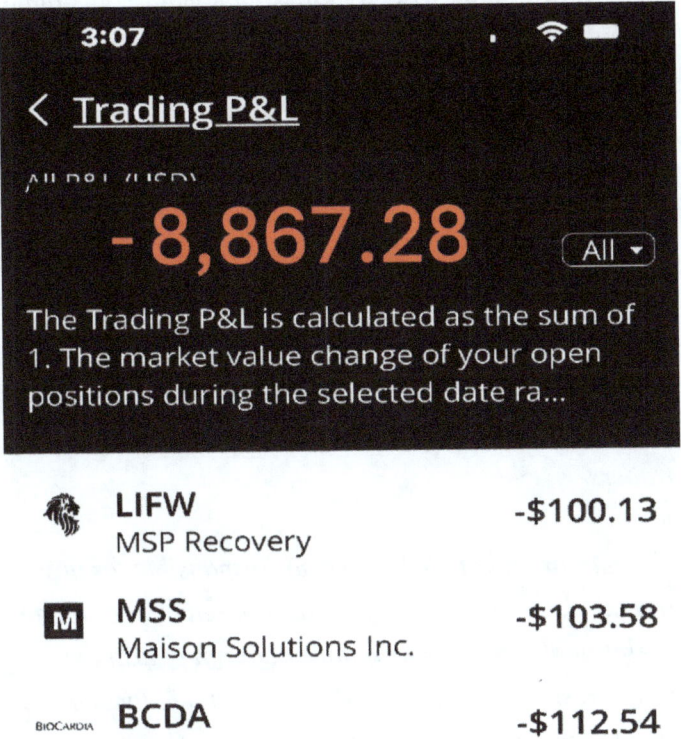

3:07

‹ Trading P&L

All P&L (USD)

-8,867.28 [All ▾]

The Trading P&L is calculated as the sum of 1. The market value change of your open positions during the selected date ra...

LIFW MSP Recovery		-$100.13
MSS Maison Solutions Inc.		-$103.58
BCDA Biocardia Inc		-$112.54

Disclaimer

The information provided in this book is for educational and informational purposes only. It is not intended as financial, investment, or trading advice, nor is it a guarantee of specific outcomes. Day trading is a high-risk activity that can result in significant financial loss. Before engaging in day trading, readers are encouraged to consult with a qualified financial advisor and conduct their own independent research. The author is not a licensed financial advisor, and any examples or strategies discussed are based on personal experiences and do not necessarily reflect the best practices for all traders.

The author and publisher are not responsible for any trading decisions made by readers based on the content of this book. Past performance does not guarantee future results. Trading involves risk, and individuals should only trade with money they can afford to lose..

DEDICATION

A SPECIAL THANK YOU TO CHUMLEY FOR THE INCREDIBLE SUPPORT THROUGHOUT THIS JOURNEY.

ACKNOWLEDGMENTS

First, I want to give a big shout-out to the Discord groups I joined during my day trading journey.

To the group leaders, thanks for your "EARTH-SHATTERING" wisdom.

To the members who lost money with me and the few brave souls who tried to help: whether you were there to answer questions or simply sit in the PIT OF DISPARE beside me - I'll always appreciate your company through this journey that MADE ME BROKE!

WHAT NOT TO DO

ENTRY AND EXIT STRATEGIES

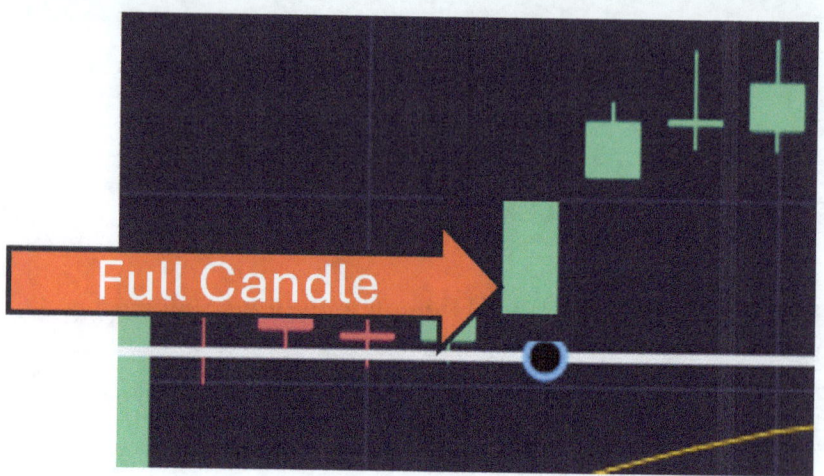

Full Candle

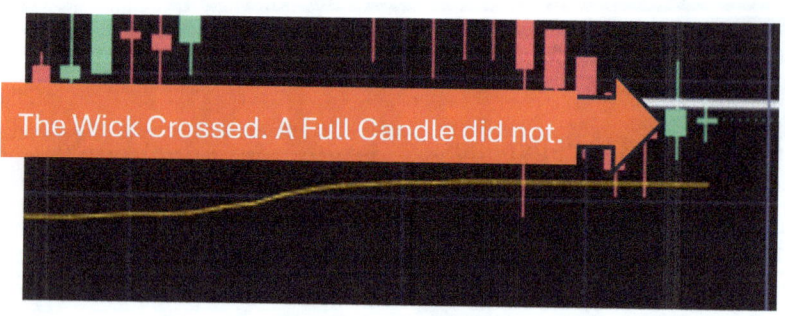

The Wick Crossed. A Full Candle did not.

ENTERING A TRADE EVEN THOUGH THE CANDLE DID NOT BREAK THE ENTRY POINT:

New traders often enter trades prematurely, thinking a stock is about to break out based on a candle's wick. Without a clear break, entering too soon can lead to losses because the price might reverse. It is best if the **candle closes above the entry** without a wick before entering the trade. Some people wait for two candles to close above the entry point.

* My winnings increased when I started waiting for a full candle to cross over the entry point.

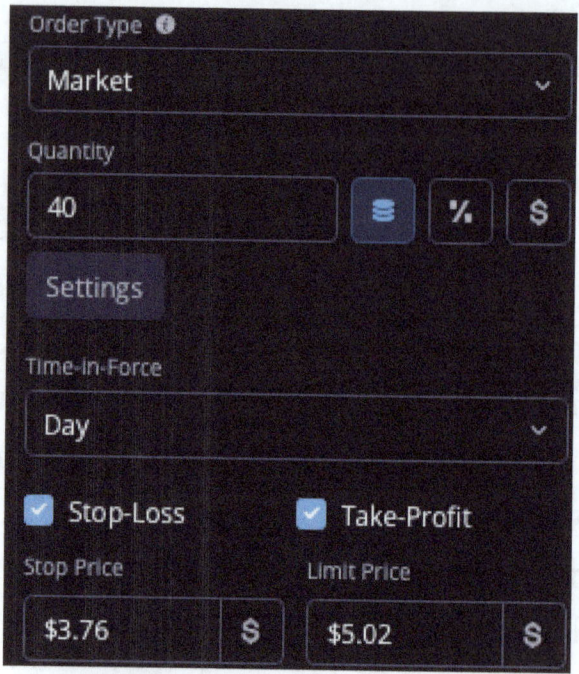

NO STOP LOSS:

Beginners often trade without setting a stop loss, risking losing far more than intended if the market turns against them.

My losses lessened when I started using the Stop Loss. Rather than losing $100 to $1000., I would only lose $15.

Be careful with the premarket if you cannot set a stop loss. I made a significant amount of money during the premarket but lost twice as much the following day during premarket due to being unable to set an SL.

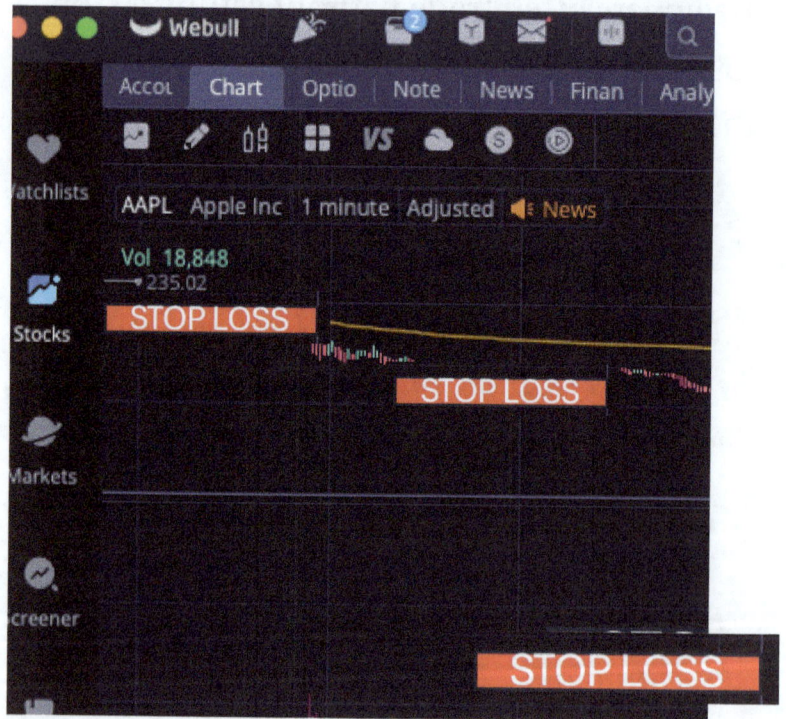

MOVING YOUR STOP LOSS:

Pushing your stop loss down can lead to much more significant losses when the stock continues in the wrong direction.

* Continuing to push my stop loss down can lead to despair.

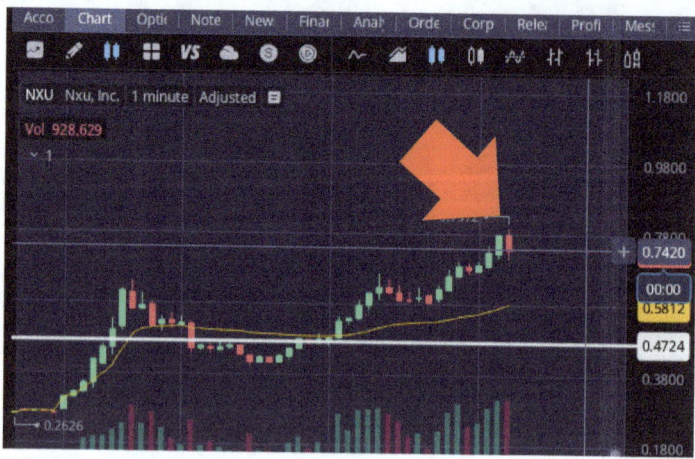

CHASING STOCKS:

Jumping into stocks after they've made big moves can result in buying near the top, only to watch them reverse.

* Chasing stocks cost me thousands!

THE COMMUNITY TELLS YOU WHEN TO GET IN AND OUT OF A TRADE, BUT YOU DON'T GET OUT:

Not following **exit instructions** from an experienced service or mentor can result in significant losses.

NOT UNDERSTANDING

your mentors' statements can be detrimental. Ex. Know what it means when a stock receives an offering.

* My winnings increased when I started following exact instructions from experienced traders.

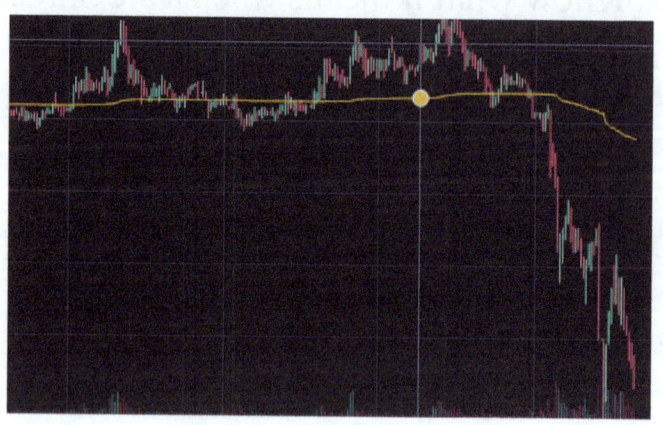

HOLDING DROPPED STOCKS OVERNIGHT - DID NOT EXIT SOON ENOUGH :

Holding day trades overnight is risky; stocks can move drastically during after-hours or pre-market sessions.

* This may be wise at times, but I'm still holding two stocks I originally intended to keep overnight. Still negative $3000. from this decision. 90% of the stocks I held overnight dropped more and did not recover.

NOT KNOWING WHEN TO BAIL:

Knowing when to exit is as crucial as entering. Beginners often hold onto losing trades too long, **HOPING** for a turnaround, which leads to more significant losses.

* Learning patterns and candlesticks, along with a strategy, helped me in regards to exiting.

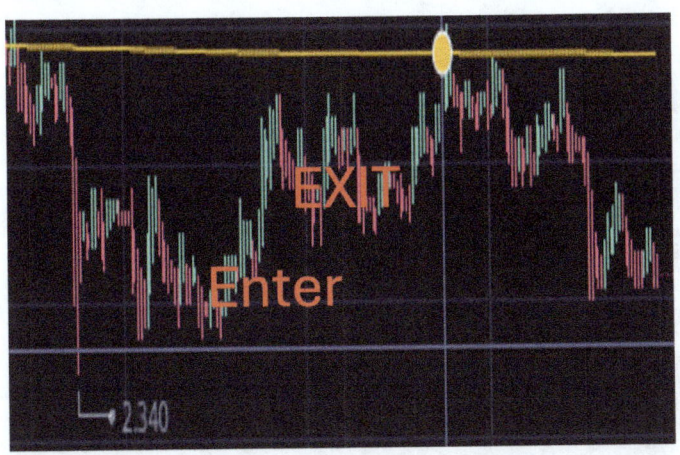

LACK OF A CLEAR STRATEGY:
Trading without a defined **strategy** that
includes entry and exit points.

**When I made the decision that I would
leave a stock if it hit negative $10., I
began to cut my losses majorly.*

TECHNICAL ANALYSIS

LACK OF UNDERSTANDING - TECHNICAL ANALYSIS:

Not knowing the basic methods for effective trading can hinder decision-making.

Key Statistics			
Open	0.7500	High	0.9400
Low	0.6827	Volume	182.59M
Prev Close	0.2503	Market Cap	10.43M
Avg Vol(3M)	264.32K	% Turnover	1,496.42%
52 Wk High	7.38	52 Wk Low	0.2089
Turnover	--	% Range	102.80%
P/E(TTM)	-0.0236	P/E Ratio(Forecast)	-0.4295
P/B	1.369	P/S	20.65
BPS	0.6276	EPS (TTM)	-36.3400
Free Float Mkt Cap	10.02M	Shares Outstanding	12.20M
Free Float	11.73M	Next Earnings	--

INTERPLAY BETWEEN VOLUME, FLOAT, AND PRICE MOVEMENT:

Failing to grasp how a stock's volume and float size affect its price movement can lead to missed opportunities and/or losses.

High	
Volume	3.23K
Prev Close	7.33
52 Wk Low	7.16
NAV	7.43
1Y Return(Cum.)	-21.49%
Div Yield	1.06%
% Range	1.36%
Lot Size	1

JUMPING IN A STOCK WITH LOW VOLUME:

Trading a stock with low volume can result in poor price execution or getting stuck in a trade.

Before I learned about volume, I made the mistake of jumping into stocks because I saw green candles moving up. Once in, the candles would stop moving upwards. There was not enough volume to keep them going. This would use up my cash. So, I was unable to make other solid plays.

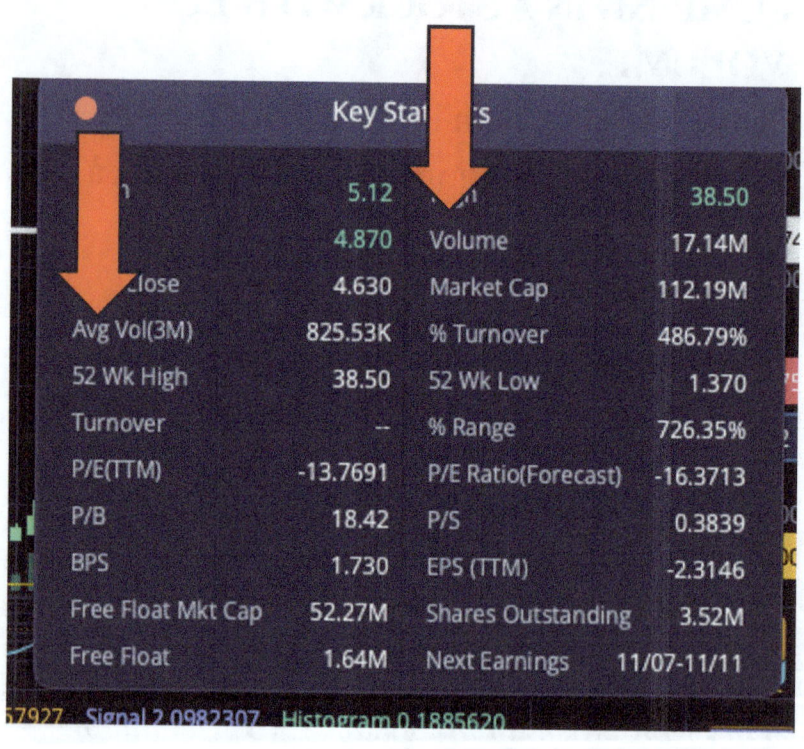

Key Statistics			
	5.12		38.50
	4.870	Volume	17.14M
Close	4.630	Market Cap	112.19M
Avg Vol(3M)	825.53K	% Turnover	486.79%
52 Wk High	38.50	52 Wk Low	1.370
Turnover	--	% Range	726.35%
P/E(TTM)	-13.7691	P/E Ratio(Forecast)	-16.3713
P/B	18.42	P/S	0.3839
BPS	1.730	EPS (TTM)	-2.3146
Free Float Mkt Cap	52.27M	Shares Outstanding	3.52M
Free Float	1.64M	Next Earnings	11/07-11/11

57927 Signal 2.0982307 Histogram 0.1885620

IMPORTANCE OF VOLUME:
Not understanding volume or where to find it can lead to poor trade execution and missed signals.

Relative Volume: Look for stocks trading at least **1.5 to 2 times their average daily volume.**

* My winnings increased once I understood and checked the volume and average volume before entering a stock. Understanding the volume prevented me from jumping into stocks prematurely.

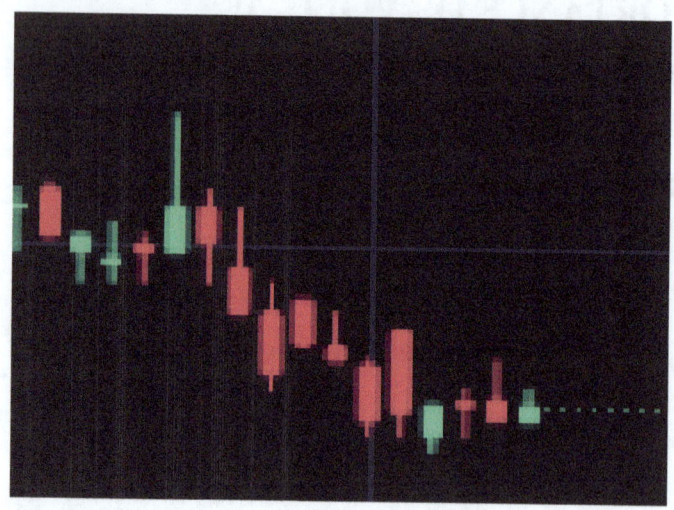

JUMPING IN A STOCK WITH BEARISH CANDLES.

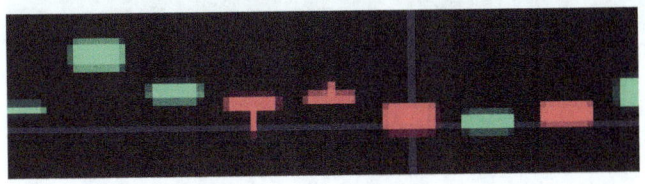

JUMPING IN A STOCK WITH LOW MOMENTUM.

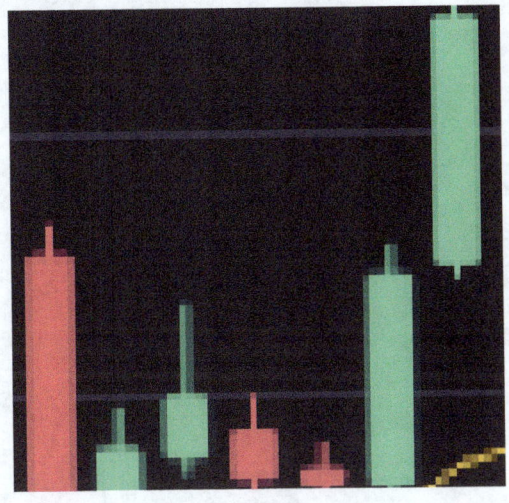

NOT UNDERSTANDING MOMENTUM:

Failing to recognize momentum can prevent traders from identifying strong price trends.

Key Statistics

Open	5.12	High	38.50
Low	4.870	Volume	17.14M
Prev Close	4.630	Market Cap	112.19M
Avg Vol(3M)	825.53K	% Turnover	486.79%
52 Wk High	38.50	52 Wk Low	1.370
Turnover	--	% Range	726.35%
P/E(TTM)	-13.7691	P/E Ratio(Forecast)	-16.3713
P/B	18.42	P/S	0.3839
BPS	1.730	EPS (TTM)	-2.3146
Free Float Mkt Cap	52.27M	Shares Outstanding	3.52M
Free Float	1.64M	Next Earnings	11/07-11/11

027 Signal 2.0......07 Histogram 0.1885620

IMPORTANCE OF STOCK FLOAT:

Not knowing how a stock's float (the number of shares available for trading) affects price changes can lead to miscalculations.

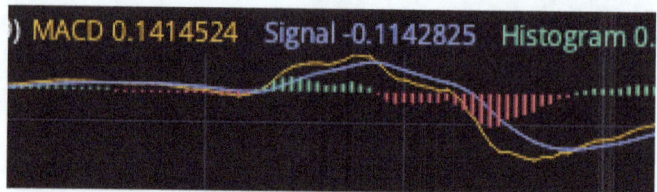

NOT USING MOVING AVERAGES:

A rising moving average indicates that the security is in an uptrend, while a declining moving average indicates a downtrend.

The 200-day moving average is considered especially significant in stock trading.

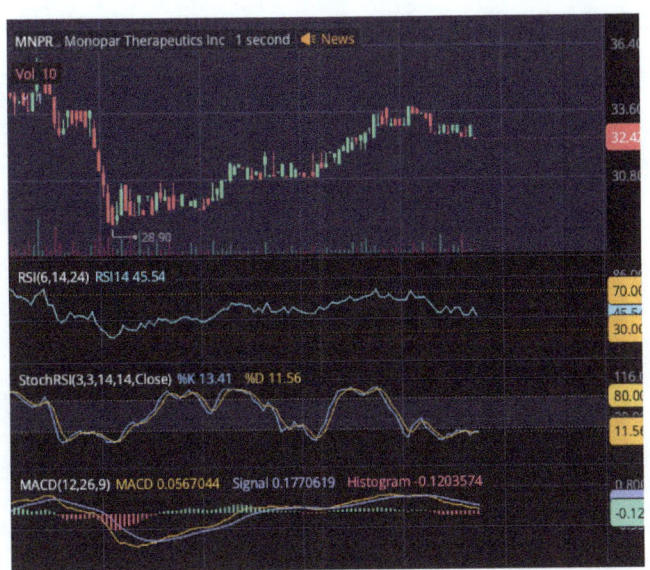

MISINTERPRETING INDICATORS:

Misreading indicators like RSI and MACD can lead to bad trading decisions.

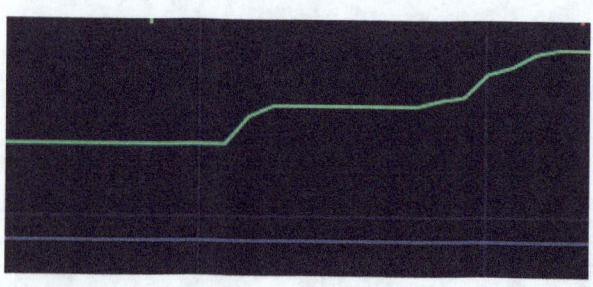

SOMETIMES, OVER-RELYING ON ONE INDICATOR:

Focusing too much on a single indicator limits overall analysis and can lead to poor trades.

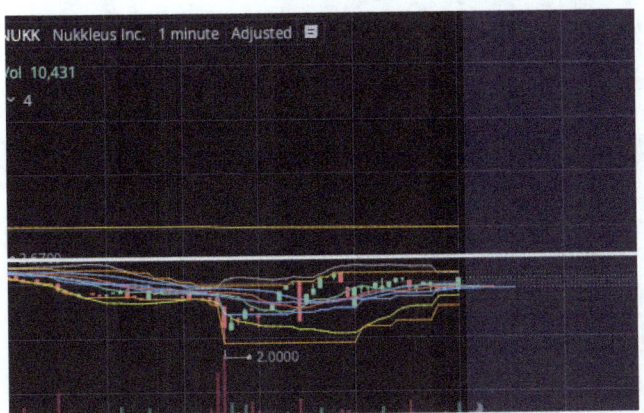

OVERCOMPLICATING ANALYSIS:
Using too many indicators or complicated strategies can confuse traders and lead to indecision.

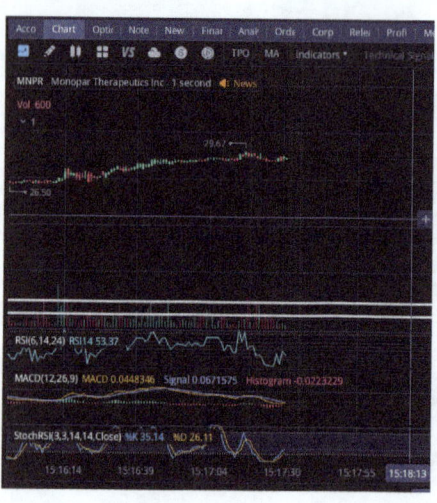

1
Minute
Chart

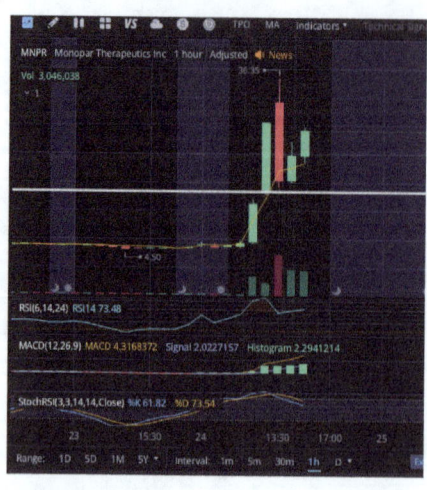

1 Hour
Chart

NOT UNDERSTANDING CHARTS:

Ignoring the different types of charts can result in poor visualization of price trends.

My winnings increased when I started comparing the 1-second chart, 1-minute chart, 5-minute chart, and the Heiken candle and regular candle.

The Double Top indicates a potential reversal.

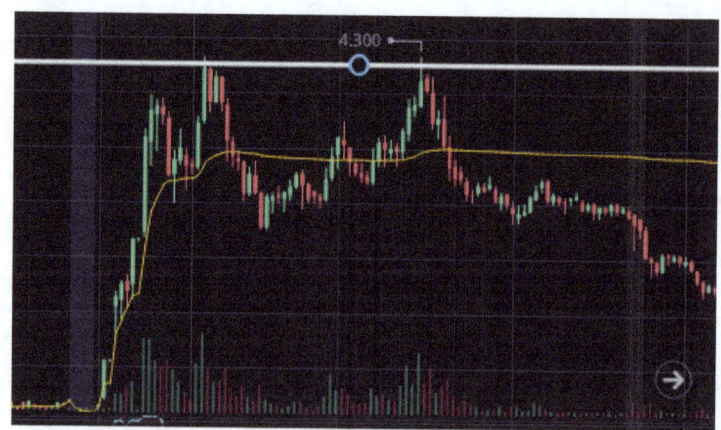

OVERLOOKING KEY PATTERNS:

Missing important chart patterns that indicate market movements can cause traders to miss profitable trades or lose a trade.

* My winnings increased just by learning a few patterns. I found the Double Top or Bottom and the Head and Shoulders easy to see.

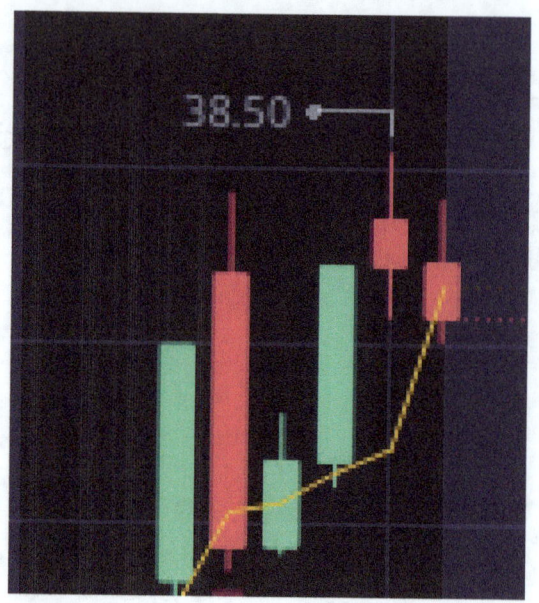

IGNORING CANDLESTICK PATTERNS:
Failing to recognize or dismiss candlestick formations can miss key signals regarding the direction of the stock going up or down in value.

INADEQUATE BACKTESTING:
Not testing strategies on historical data can result in strategies that don't work in real (live) trading.

TOOLS

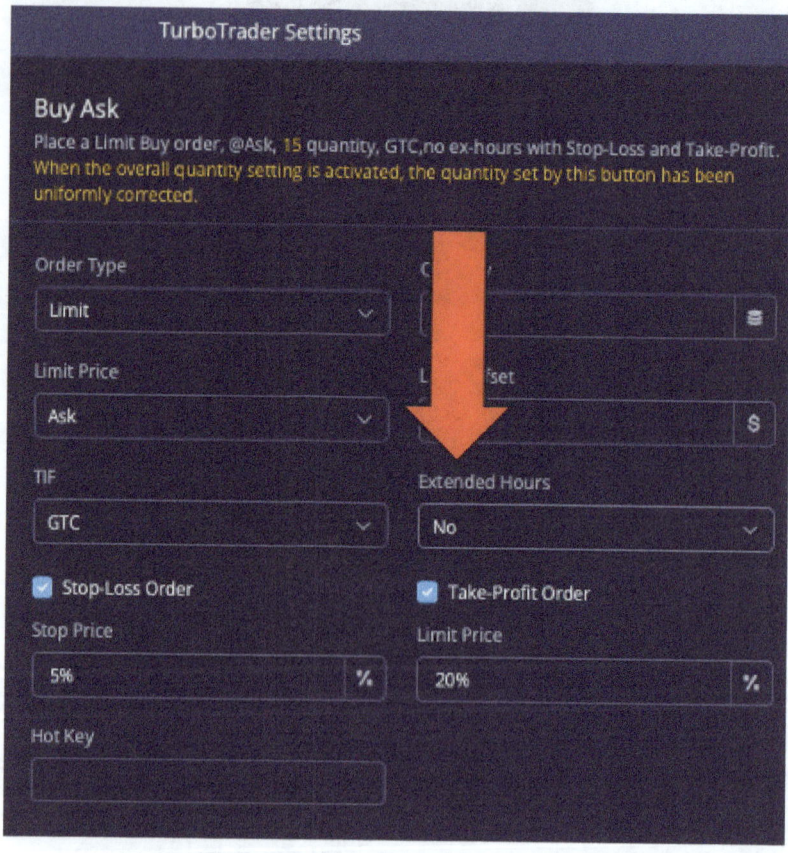

TurboTrader Settings

Buy Ask

Place a Limit Buy order, @Ask, 15 quantity, GTC,no ex-hours with Stop-Loss and Take-Profit. When the overall quantity setting is activated, the quantity set by this button has been uniformly corrected.

Order Type			
Limit			

Limit Price

Ask

TIF

GTC

Extended Hours

No

☑ Stop-Loss Order

Stop Price

5% %

☑ Take-Profit Order

Limit Price

20% %

Hot Key

INCORRECT TURBO TRADER SETTINGS IN PRE-MARKET:

Not setting up turbo trader software properly for pre-market trading can lead to issues like delayed orders or buying at the wrong price. Check your settings before you begin trading.

A couple of times, I missed great trades because I did not have "Extended Hours" set to yes.

NO HOT KEY:

Not having pre-set hotkeys can slow execution in fast-moving markets.

Always have a quick escape.

TRADING EXECUTION

IMPULSE TRADING:

Jumping into stocks without following your rules can lead to losses.

NOT SETTING RULES TO FOLLOW NOR STICKING WITH THEM FOR CONSISTENCY IN TRADING.

* My winnings increased when my rules were followed. Ex. SL at -5%.

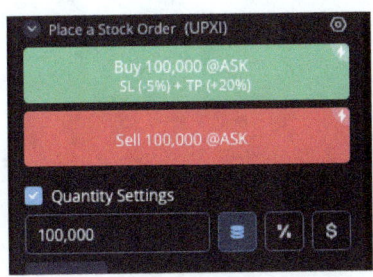

ACCIDENTALLY HITTING A BUY OR SELL BUTTON.

RELYING TOO HEAVILY ON PAID SERVICES:

Depending on paid services without learning.

EMOTIONAL AND PSYCHOLOGICAL FACTORS

GREED:

Many traders chase profits, staying in trades longer than they should, which can result in holding through a reversal and losing profits.

NO SELF-CONTROL:
Emotional trading leads to poor decision-making and losses.

I found self-control to be one of the most important rules.   When I stopped jumping into stocks I saw moving fast ., mu losses reduced majorly

DESPERATE:

When you play the stock market out of desperation, emotions cloud your judgment, leading to impulsive decisions and often costly mistakes.

REVENGE TRADING:
Trying to quickly recover losses from a
bad trade by making impulsive and often
riskier trades.

FOMO (FEAR OF MISSING OUT):
Entering trades out of fear of missing potential profits can lead to jumping into volatile or overvalued stocks at the wrong time. There will always be another trade! Wait for it!

OVERTRADING:
Making too many trades in a short period out of excitement or revenge leads to unnecessary fees and losses.

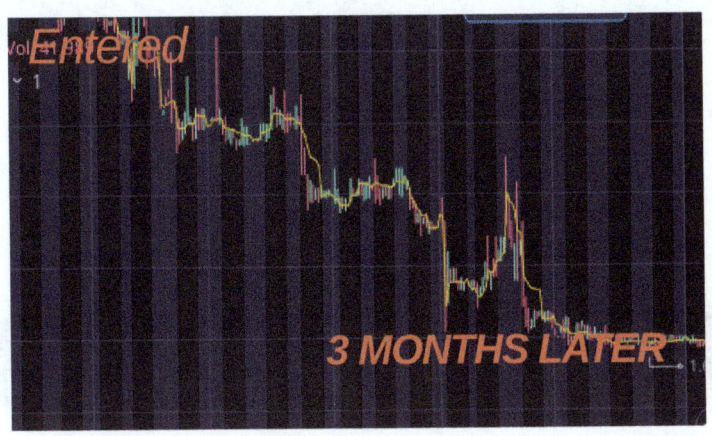

HOLDING ON RATHER THAN SELLING WHEN REVERSES:

Refusing to sell losing trades, hoping the market will turn around, can lead to even more significant losses if the stock continues to drop.

MARKET AWARENESS

News

S&P 500

Bankruptcy

The Dow Jones

Merger

Nasdaq

Acquisition

Catastrophic Events

IGNORING MARKET CONDITIONS:
Analyzing patterns without accounting for the broader market environment can lead to **costly mistakes.**

NOT FINDING STOCKS WITH A CATALYST:
Overlooking stocks with potential news or events (catalysts) that could drive prices higher can lead to missed trading opportunities.

Examples: Campbell soup stock increased during the depression. Healthcare stocks increased during covid.

* My winnings increased when I only played stocks based on the news.

RISK MANAGEMENT

Balance

100.00

Buying 100.00 in a stock to day trade

POOR RISK MANAGEMENT:

Risking too much on a single trade without considering overall capital at risk can lead to significant losses. For a general rule, some traders may risk up to 1%–2% of their account on a single trade.

MISCELLANEOUS

Your **COMPUTER FREEZES** because you left it on for a few days. Be sure to turn your computer off and on before you begin. Some people turn on two computers.

NOT KEEPING A TRADING JOURNAL.
Failing to document trades and analyze performance makes learning from mistakes and improving over time harder.

Trading P&L

Total P&L (USD): -$19,244.52   [MAX ▼]

Symbol	Name	P&L
VS	Versus Systems Inc	-582.12
ASTI	Ascent Solar Tec	-742.94
ICCT	iCoreConnect Inc.	-778.46
AGRI	Agriforce Growing Systems Ltd	-793.44
LQR	LQR House Inc.	-887.33
INM	Inmed Pharmaceuticals Inc	-906.56
ELAB	Elevai Labs, Inc.	-1,173.74
VINO	Gaucho Group Hldgs Inc	-1,345.89
HURA	TuHURA Biosciences	-1,367.56
SYTA	Siyata Mobile Inc	-1,490.76
IFBD	Infobird Co Ltd	-2,570.11
ABVC	Abvc Biopharma Inc	-2,660.26

Trading P&L

Total P&L (USD): -$19,244.52   [MAX ▼]

Symbol	Name	P&L
FEMY	FEMASYS INC	+856.00
AMZN	Amazon Com	+511.75
GOOGL	Alphabet Inc	+463.62
ROII	RiskOn International	+378.17
BXRXQ	Baudax Bio Inc	+356.23
MSFT	Microsoft Corp	+283.80
SNGX	Soligenix Inc	+275.29
ICU	SeaStar Medical Holding Corp	+272.98
NIVF	NewGenIvf Group	+255.16
TTOO	T2 Biosystems	+253.60
AAPL	Apple Inc	+238.39
CISO	Ciso Global	+200.56

THINKING YOU CAN MAKE THE SAME AMOUNT OF MONEY YOU LOST IN THE SAME AMOUNT OF TIME OR, MAKE AS MUCH AS YOU LOSE IN GENERAL.

It's very easy to lose $1000 on a stock. It can be challenging to make $30.

The most I made on a trade was $856.
The most I lost was $2660. I sold assuming I could easily make that amount with another stock.

The most I made on a stock was $856. The most I lost on a stock was over $2600.

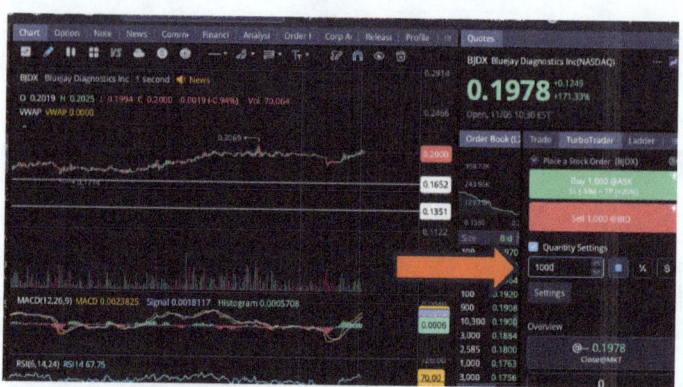

.1978 x 1000= $197.80

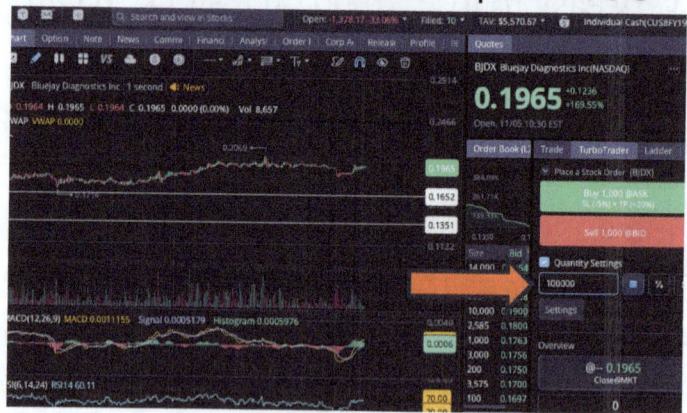

.1978 x 100000= $19,780

MISCALCULATING THE NUMBER OF STOCKS PURCHASED CAN BE COSTLY ESPECIALLY IF THE STOCK DROPS FAST.

*Double-check the total cost of the shares you're buying. Miscalculating the cost of the "quantity" I entered ended up increasing my losses.

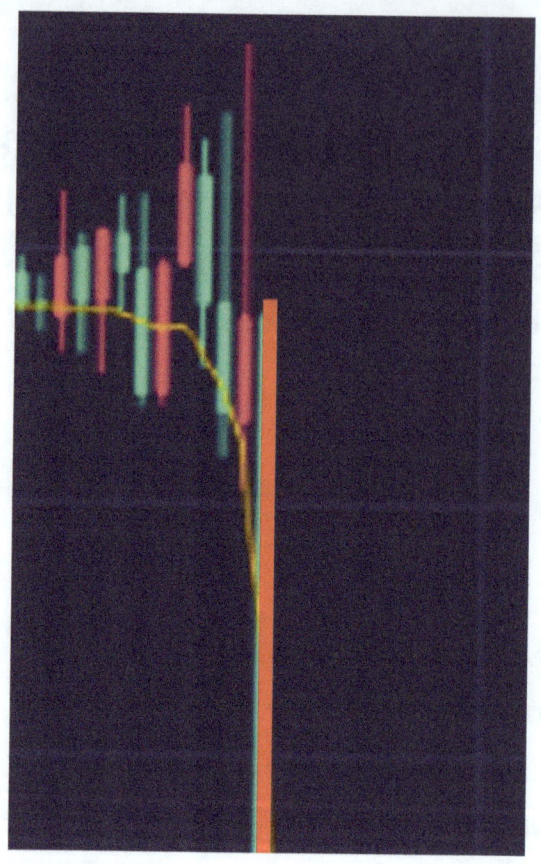

STOCKS DROPPING FAST!

* Be aware. It happens.

SCATTERED BRAIN.
NOT FOCUSED. OVERWHELMED.

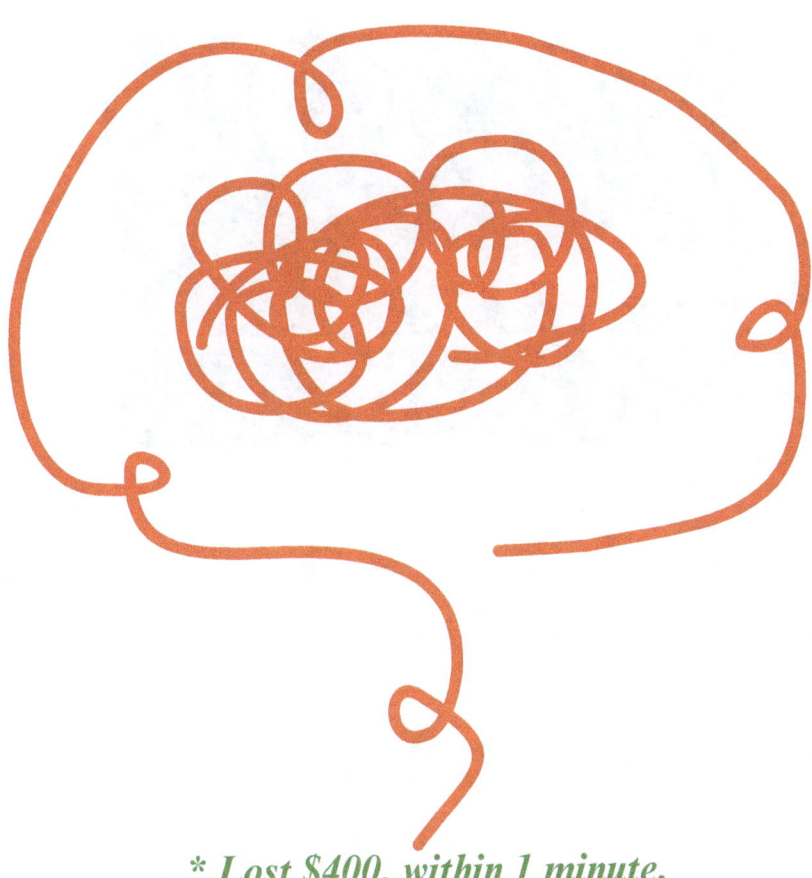

* Lost $400. within 1 minute.

MOST EXPENSIVE MISTAKES

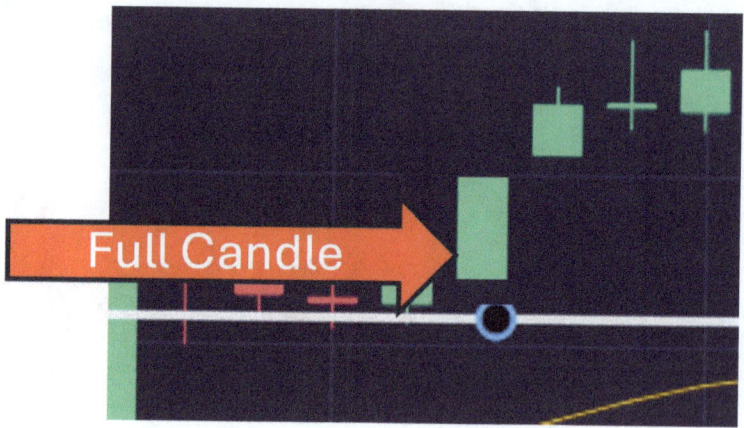

Full Candle

MOST
EXPENSIVE MISTAKES

Entering a trade even though
the Candle Did Not Break
the Entry Point.

MOST EXPENSIVE MISTAKES

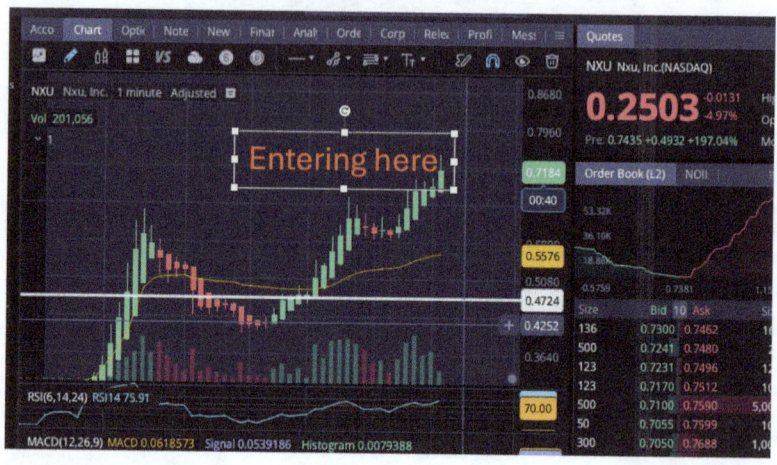

MOST EXPENSIVE MISTAKES

Chasing Stocks: Jumping into stocks after they've made big moves can result in buying near the top, only to watch them reverse. **(Lack of Self-Control!)**

MOST
EXPENSIVE MISTAKES

Breaking my Rules.

Good Luck!